The Usborne First Encyclopedia of Seas and Oceans

Ben Denne

Designed by Nelupa Hussain
and Helen Wood
Illustrated by David Hancock

Consultants: Dr. Margaret Rostron, Dr. John Rostron,
John Davidson and H.M. Hignett
Managing editor: Felicity Brooks
Managing designer: Mary Cartwright
Digital manipulation: John Russell
Cover design: Laura Fearn

SCHOLASTIC INC.
New York   Toronto   London   Auckland   Sydney
Mexico City   New Delhi   Hong Kong   Buenos Aires

Using Internet links – notes for parents and teachers

It's quick and easy to access the Web sites described in this book using Usborne Quicklinks. Just go to **www.usborne-quicklinks.com** and follow the instructions there. Here are some of the things children can do on the Web sites recommended in this book:

• Design a fish

• Hear what a whale sounds like

• See barnacles feeding

• Go to a sailor school

• Solve a food web mystery

With each recommended Web site there is a brief description of what can be found there.

What you need

Most of the Web sites described in this book can be accessed with a standard home computer and an Internet browser (the software that lets you display information from the Internet). Some sites need extra programs (plug-ins) to play sounds, show videos, animations or 3-D images. If you go to a site and do not have the necessary plug-in, a message will come up on the screen. There is usually a button on the site that you can click on to download the plug-in. Alternatively, go to Usborne Quicklinks and click on **Net Help**. There you can find links to download plug-ins.

Downloadable pictures

Pictures in this book that have the ★ symbol next to them can be downloaded from Usborne Quicklinks and printed out free of charge, for use in homework and projects, for example. The pictures must not be copied or distributed for any commercial purpose. To find the pictures go to **www.usborne-quicklinks.com** and follow the instructions there.

COMPUTER NOT ESSENTIAL
This book is a complete, superb, self-contained information book by itself.

Internet safety

All the sites described in this book have been selected by Usborne editors as suitable, in their opinion, for children, although no guarantees can be given and Usborne Publishing is not responsible for the accuracy or suitability of the information on any Web site other than its own. **We recommend that young children are supervised while on the Internet, and that children do not use Internet chat rooms.**

Site availability

Occasionally a site is unavailable. This may be temporary, so try again later. Some Web site addresses may change or sites may close down. The links on the Usborne Quicklinks Web site are regularly updated to send you to the right place, or to suitable alternative sites.

Help

For general help and advice go to Usborne Quicklinks and click on **Net Help**. You'll find a brief guide to using the Internet and the software you need, as well as links to other helpful sites.

Notes for children

• Always check with a parent, teacher, or the owner of the computer that it is all right to connect to the Internet.

• Never give out information about yourself, such as your real name, address or phone number.

• Never arrange to meet someone you come across on the Internet.

For access to the Web sites described in this book and for free, downloadable pictures, go to

www.usborne-quicklinks.com

Contents

4 Seas and oceans
6 Underwater life
8 Who eats who?
10 Hiding
12 Coral reefs
14 Coral reef animals
16 Living together
18 Poisonous animals
20 Sharks
22 Rays
24 Whales
26 Dolphins
28 Deep down
30 On the move
32 Cold oceans
34 Waves
36 Currents
37 Tides
38 Coasts
40 Seashore life
42 Dangerous seas
44 Boats and ships
46 Exploring the depths
47 Unknown seas

48 Shipwrecks
50 Using the oceans
52 Dirty oceans
54 Emptying the oceans
56 Getting warmer
58 The future of the oceans
60 Undersea facts and records
62 Index

Seas and oceans

Seas and oceans cover more than two-thirds of the Earth. They make our planet look blue from space. There are five different oceans. In the oceans are lots of smaller areas of salty water, which are called seas.

Watery world

It is like a different world under the oceans. There are deep valleys, huge mountains, forests of seaweed and many amazing sea animals.

Internet link

At **www.usborne-quicklinks.com** you'll find a link to the **Ocean Planet Web site**, where you can find out fascinating facts about the oceans.

Coast

Oil rig

Divers only go down to about 150m (500ft). The deepest part of the oceans is more than 80 times deeper than this.

Most oceans have a shallow area near the coast, called a continental shelf.

Oil gets trapped between layers of rock under the sea.

People use oil from under the seabed to make fuel. See page 51 to find out more.

The bottom of the sea is called the seabed.

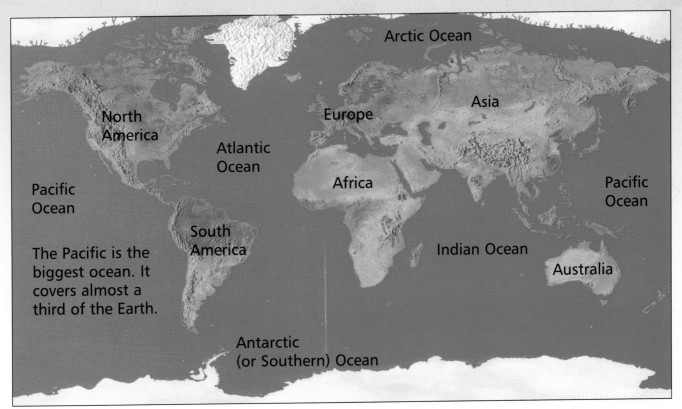

This map of the world shows the five different oceans. Remember that the world is really round, so the two parts of the Pacific Ocean are joined up.

Arctic Ocean

Asia

Europe

North America

Atlantic Ocean

Africa

Pacific Ocean

Pacific Ocean

The Pacific is the biggest ocean. It covers almost a third of the Earth.

South America

Indian Ocean

Australia

Antarctic (or Southern) Ocean

Some islands are the tops of enormous undersea mountains.

Undersea volcanoes throw out boiling melted rock called lava.

Darkest depths

The deepest place in any ocean is the Mariana Trench in the Pacific. If you dropped a 1kg (2.2lb) rock into the water there, it would take over an hour to reach the seabed.

The Petronas Towers is one of the world's tallest buildings. 28 of them standing on top of each other in the Mariana Trench wouldn't reach the surface of the water.

The bottom of the deep trenches are completely dark, but some animals live down there.

5

Underwater life

The oceans are full of plants and animals. Here are some of the things you can find out about in this book.

Internet link

At **www.usborne-quicklinks.com** you'll find a link to the **Virtual Fishtank Web site**, where you can design your own fish.

Sharks are fierce hunters. You can find out all about them on pages 20-21.

Find out all about dolphins on pages 26-27.

Read about coral reefs and the animals that live on them on pages 12-15.

Sea slugs collect other animals' poison. Read about them on page 19.

What are fish?

Fish are a group of animals that live in water. There are thousands of different kinds. They come in different shapes and sizes, but they all have gills and fins. Gills allow them to breathe underwater, and fins help them to move around.

Caudal fin

Most fish have flat tails, which they move from side to side to swim. Their strong tail muscles make swimming easy.

Fish use these top fins, called dorsal fins, to help keep their balance.

This flap, called the operculum, covers the fish's gills.

Pelvic fins help fish to change direction quickly.

Fish use these fins, called pectoral fins, for turning.

This line, called the lateral line, helps fish to sense movement in the water.

Slimy skin helps fish to move easily through water.

Breathing

Fish breathe by taking oxygen out of the water. Here's how they do it.

Gills under here

As a fish moves forward, it takes in water through its mouth. The water passes over its gills.

The fish's gills take oxygen from the water. The water then passes out under the fish's operculum.

Fish scales

Most fish are protected by a covering of tiny plates, called scales. These scales are waterproof, and help to protect the fish from pests and hunters.

Fish scales overlap each other, to make a protective cover.

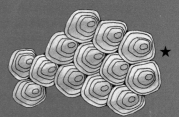

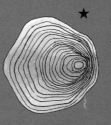

The rings on a fish's scales show how old the fish is. Some fish can live for up to 80 years.

Who eats who?

The animals in the oceans depend on each other to survive. Some animals eat plants, but some hunt and eat other animals.

Hunters and hunted

Animals which hunt and eat other animals are known as predators. The animals that they eat are called prey.

This killer whale is a predator. It is hunting mackerel. The mackerel are its prey.

Drifting plankton

Plankton are animals and plants which provide food for lots of other animals. There are billions of them in the oceans. They cannot swim, so they drift through the water. Most kinds of plankton are tiny.

Tiny plants in the water, such as these diatoms, are called phytoplankton.

One glass of sea water can contain as many as 50,000 phytoplankton.

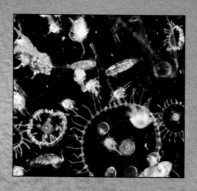

These zooplankton animals are shown larger than they really are. In real life, most of them are actually smaller than one of the letters in these words.

Web of life

Food webs, like this one, show who eats who. The arrows point from the prey to the predators. Most predators are also prey for other, bigger animals. Predators which aren't eaten by other animals are called top predators.

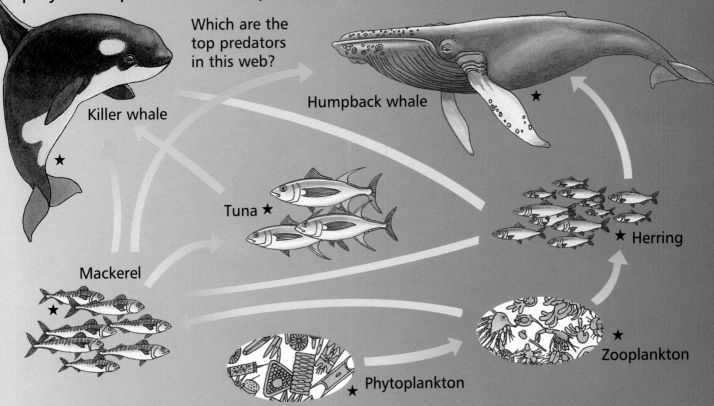

Which are the top predators in this web?

Killer whale ★

Humpback whale ★

Tuna ★

Herring ★

Mackerel ★

Zooplankton ★

Phytoplankton ★

New from old

When animals are eaten by other animals, they pass on energy. Even if they die of old age, the energy is still passed on through the food web. When they die, animals help create new life. Follow the numbers to see how this happens.

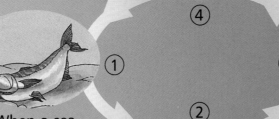

① 1. When a sea animal dies, it sinks to the seabed and gets covered in mud.

② 2. In the mud are tiny living things called bacteria. They feed on the remains of the dead animal.

③ 3. Bacteria break the remains down into separate parts called nutrients, and release them back into the water.

④ 4. Plankton use the nutrients to build their bodies, which sea animals eat before they die.

Internet link

At **www.usborne-quicklinks.com** you'll find a link to the **What Eats What Web site,** where you can find out about a different kind of food web.

9

Hiding

Many sea animals are difficult to spot because the patterns on their bodies look like their surroundings. This is called camouflage. Camouflage helps animals to hide when they are in danger. It can also help predators sneak up on prey.

Sea dragons have lots of leafy parts on their bodies, to make them look like seaweed.

Wobbegong sharks have flat bodies. They lie on the seabed, and snap up fish that swim past.

Flatfish disguise

Some flatfish use the seabed for camouflage. They cover themselves in sand and lie very still so they won't be seen.

Can you see the fish in this picture?

Safe spines

Shrimpfish hide by hanging head-down among the spines of sea urchins. The stripes along the sides of their bodies make them look like one of the sea urchin's spines. This protects them from predators.

Can you see the shrimpfish hiding on this sea urchin?

Changing patterns

Cuttlefish hunt on the seabed, eating fish and crabs. They have long tentacles which dart out to catch their prey. As they pass over different areas, their body pattern changes completely, to match their surroundings.

This cuttlefish is camouflaged against the sand.

As it moves over some rocks, its pattern changes.

Fierce frogfish

Sargassum frogfish live in areas of floating sargassum seaweed. Their bodies are perfectly camouflaged to look like the seaweed. They stay very still, and wait for their prey to swim close to them.

A sargassum frogfish can use its front fins like hands to cling to the seaweed.

Coral reefs

Corals live in warm, shallow seas. Although they look like plants, corals are really made of thousands of small animals. Large areas of coral are called coral reefs.

Internet link

At **www.usborne-quicklinks.com** you'll find a link to the **Seasky Web site**, where you can learn about lots of different kinds of corals.

Angelfish live among corals. Their bright markings help them blend in with their surroundings.

Coral animals

Coral animals are protected by hard skeletons. When they die, their skeletons are left behind. New coral animals grow on top of them so that over time, a coral reef slowly forms.

There are four fish and an eel hiding in this coral reef. Can you spot them all?

A coral animal, cut in half.

Poisonous tentacles for catching food

Mouth

Stomach

Stony base

Sea fan

Sponge

Sea urchin

Brittle star

Brain coral

Reef life

Coral reefs are full of nooks and crannies where animals can hide and make their homes. This means there is always lots of sea life around them.

A coral meal

The animals in coral are well-protected by their shells, but some fish such as parrotfish are able to eat them.

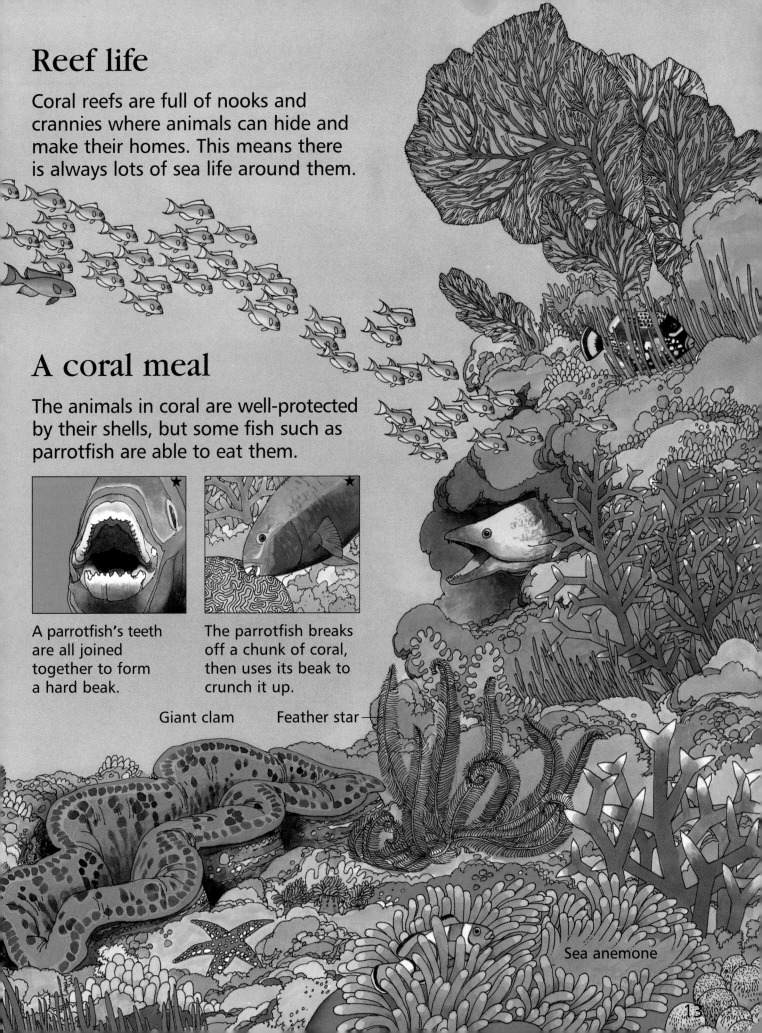

A parrotfish's teeth are all joined together to form a hard beak.

The parrotfish breaks off a chunk of coral, then uses its beak to crunch it up.

Giant clam

Feather star

Sea anemone

13

Coral reef animals

More than a quarter of all the creatures in the sea live around coral reefs. This includes animals of all shapes and sizes, and more than 2,000 kinds of fish.

Octopuses can squirt ink into the water if they are attacked. This makes the water cloudy, helping them to escape.

Clown triggerfish swim over the coral eating tiny animals, such as worms, which live on it.

Giant groupers are the biggest coral reef predators. They can grow to the length of a small car.

Internet link

At **www.usborne-quicklinks.com** you'll find a link to the **Seasky Web site**, where you can learn about all the different animals living around coral reefs.

Angelfish eat sponges, which live on the coral.

Seahorses live among corals. They swim by moving the fin on their backs.

Safe on the reef

Coral reefs are home to fierce predators such as sharks, so reef animals need to have ways of protecting themselves. Some have patterns which make them look scary. Others have stranger tricks.

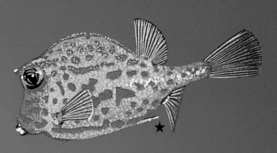

Pufferfish blow themselves up when they are frightened, to scare off predators.

Boxfish are covered in a foul-tasting slime, which protects them from predators.

Predators may think the spot on this butterfly fish's back is the eye of a really big fish.

Safe in schools

Some fish swim in big groups called schools. This helps confuse predators, so they don't know which fish to attack. They might even think the whole school is a much bigger animal.

These crescent-tailed bigeye fish are swimming close together in a school.

Living together

Some sea creatures need help from other animals to survive. This is called symbiosis. Usually symbiosis is good for both animals, but sometimes it only helps one of them.

Long, thin fish called remoras often cling to bigger animals such as this green turtle. They feed on leftover scraps from the bigger animals' meals.

Living home

Pearlfish use other animals for protection by living inside them. Sometimes they start to eat the animals they live in from the inside.

This pearlfish is living inside a sea cucumber. It gets in and out through the sea cucumber's breathing hole.

Safe from stings

Anemones eat little fish. They have stinging tentacles to kill fish which swim into them. Clownfish live among these tentacles but the poison doesn't harm them. This keeps them safe from enemies, which get stung when they swim too close.

Clownfish are covered in a slime which protects them from the anemone's poison.

Goby watchman

Some kinds of shrimp are nearly blind. These shrimp live with fish called gobies, and the two animals help each other. The shrimp build safe burrows for both animals to live in, and in return the gobies watch out for predators.

A shrimp builds a burrow with its strong claws, which both animals live in.

When they are outside, the shrimp keeps a feeler on the goby's tail.

If the goby senses danger, it swishes its tail. Both animals quickly hide in the burrow.

Pest control

Cleaner fish live on coral reefs. They swim around bigger fish, picking off dead skin and pests. Sometimes bigger fish, such as these groupers, line up to get cleaned. Cleaner fish wriggle their bodies so that the fish they clean recognize them, and don't eat them.

Sometimes bigger fish let cleaner fish into their mouths to clean their teeth and gills.

Underwater dentist

Banded coral shrimp use their long, sharp claws to clean other animals skin and teeth. They eat the bits of food they find. The bigger animals know they are helping, and don't try to eat them.

This banded coral shrimp is picking bits of food from a moray eel's teeth.

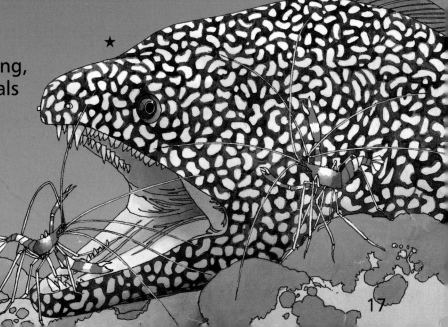

Poisonous animals

Some of the most poisonous animals in the world live in the sea. They use poison to catch their prey, or to protect themselves from enemies.

These animals all have deadly poison, and can kill people.

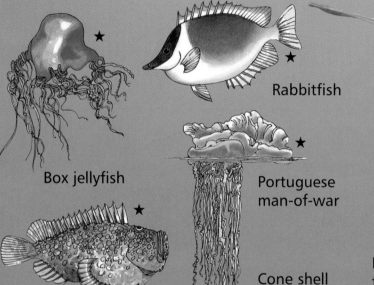

Rabbitfish ★

Box jellyfish

Portuguese man-of-war ★

Cone shell ★

Stonefish ★

Lionfish are covered with spines, which are filled with poison.

Small but deadly

The blue-ringed octopus has a deadly poison in its bite which stops its prey from breathing. Blue-ringed octopus bites have even killed people.

Blue-ringed octopus (actual size). The blue rings warn predators that the octopus is poisonous. ★

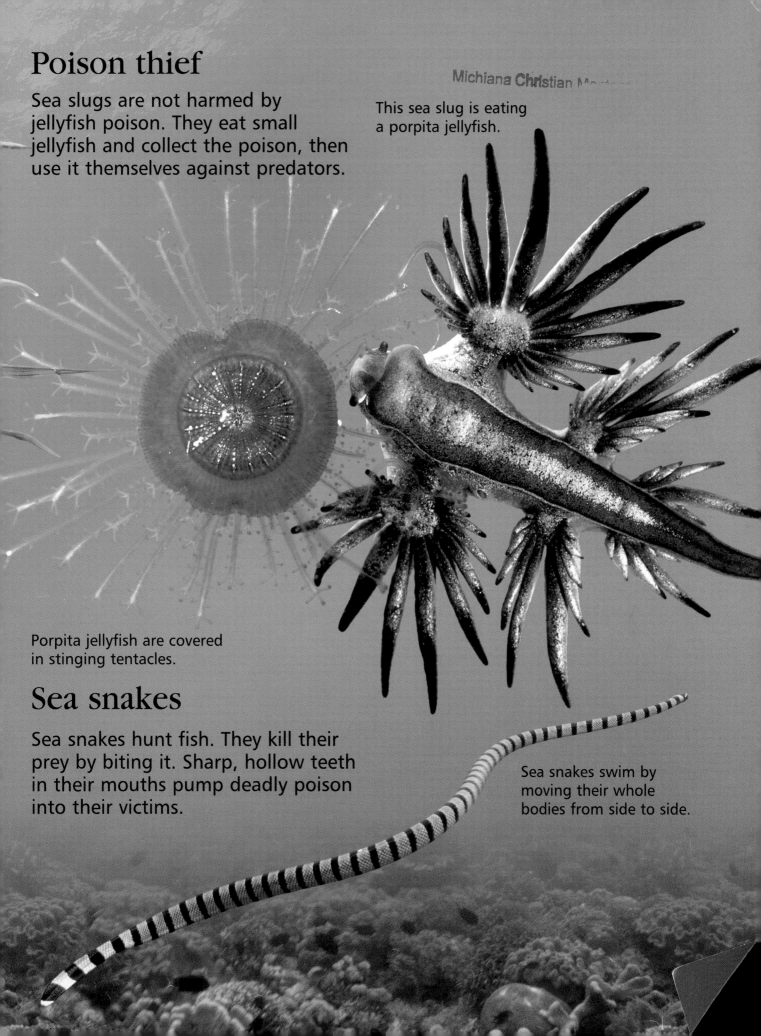

Poison thief

Sea slugs are not harmed by jellyfish poison. They eat small jellyfish and collect the poison, then use it themselves against predators.

This sea slug is eating a porpita jellyfish.

Porpita jellyfish are covered in stinging tentacles.

Sea snakes

Sea snakes hunt fish. They kill their prey by biting it. Sharp, hollow teeth in their mouths pump deadly poison into their victims.

Sea snakes swim by moving their whole bodies from side to side.

Sharks

Sharks are fish which live in oceans all over the world. There are more than 300 different kinds. Most are fierce hunters, with sharp teeth for catching and killing other animals.

Internet link

At **www.usborne-quicklinks.com** you'll find a link to the **Enchanted Learning Web site**, where you can find out about all kinds of sharks, including prehistoric ones.

Whale sharks are not a danger to people. Divers can swim with them safely.

People killers?

Great white sharks like to surprise their prey from below and kill it with only one bite, to save energy. They sometimes attack swimmers, but scientists believe they do this by mistake, thinking that humans are other sea animals.

Great white shark

Great white sharks kill their prey by biting it. They can open their mouths very wide.

As their mouths open, their teeth point forward, helping them to take a bigger bite.

Whale sharks are the world's biggest fish. They can grow up to 12m (40ft) long.

Hammerhead sharks have eyes on each end of a long flat head. This helps them to see all around as they swim.

Sharks swim by moving their tails from side to side.

Mystery fin

Sharks, like dolphins and whales, sometimes swim near the surface of the sea with their dorsal (back) fins sticking out of the water. Which of these do you think is a shark's fin? (Answer below)

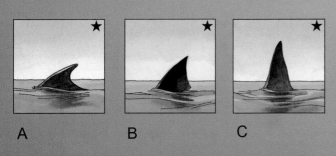

A   B   C

A is a dolphin's fin, B is the shark's fin, and C is a killer whale's fin.

Hundreds of teeth

Most sharks have at least three rows of teeth. As they lose the ones in front, teeth from the rows behind move forward to replace them.

A sand tiger shark's teeth point back so that fish it catches can't wriggle free.

Rays

There are hundreds of different kinds of rays. They all have flat bodies. Some are harmless, but stingrays can give a poisonous sting from their tails and electric rays can give an electric shock. They do this to protect themselves if they are attacked.

You can see the poisonous spine on the end of this stingray's tail.

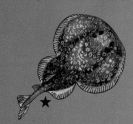

Organs on the sides of an electric ray's head can give a powerful shock.

These huge manta rays are swimming in a school.

Feeding

Most rays have their mouths on the underneath of their bodies. They swim along the seabed, eating things they swim over and can crunch up shells with their teeth to get to the animals inside.

This picture shows the underneath of a ray. The position of its mouth helps it to feed on the seabed.

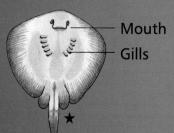

Mouth

Gills

Internet link

At **www.usborne-quicklinks.com** you'll find a link to the **Enchanted Learning Web site**, where you can find out all about rays.

Stingrays move along the seabed by rippling their fins.

Manta rays

The biggest kinds of rays are manta rays. They can be up to 6m (20ft) across, but are not dangerous. They feed by swimming slowly with their mouths open, eating plankton and other tiny animals floating in the water.

These flaps, called cephalic lobes, help to push food into the ray's mouth.

Divers sometimes swim with manta rays. You can find out about diving on page 48.

★

★

★

Manta rays swim by moving their fins up and down, like enormous wings.

23

Whales

Whales are the biggest animals in the world. They look like fish, but whales are actually mammals. Mammals are warm-blooded. This means that however hot or cold their surroundings are, their body temperature always stays the same.

Blue whales are the heaviest animals on Earth. A fully grown blue whale can weigh as much as 20 elephants.

Humpback whale

Blue whale

Right whale

Sperm whale

Minke whale

Spout shapes

Mammals cannot breathe underwater, so whales have to come to the surface of the ocean to breathe. They breathe through holes on top of their heads called blowholes. When they breathe out, they shoot out sprays of water. This is called spouting.

Different whales spout in different ways. By looking at the shape of a whale's spout, you can tell what kind of whale it is.

Sperm whales are the deepest diving whales, and can hold their breath for over an hour. They dive deep to catch giant squid to eat.

Internet link

At **www.usborne-quicklinks.com** you'll find a link to the **Whale Acoustics Project Web site**, where you can find out what whales sound like.

Energetic whales

Even though they are huge, whales can be very energetic. Big whales, such as humpback whales, often throw themselves right out of the water. This is called breaching. Nobody knows exactly why they do it.

Whales might breach to try to knock off barnacles, which cling to their skin.

Whales often throw their tails in the air when they dive. This is called fluking, and helps them dive deep.

25

Dolphins

Dolphins are mammals that live in oceans all over the world. They often live in big groups. They are some of the most intelligent animals in the sea.

A group of dolphins is called a school. Some schools contain over a hundred dolphins.

Internet link

At **www.usborne-quicklinks.com** you'll find a link to the **Ocean Link Web site,** where you can find answers to all your questions about dolphins.

Learning to breathe

Dolphins breathe air, so when a baby dolphin is born, its mother must quickly push it to the surface of the sea and teach it to breathe, or else it will drown. Sometimes, another dolphin helps her do this.

This dolphin has just had a baby. Now the baby must learn how to breathe.

The mother swims under her baby, and gently pushes it up.

The baby takes its first breath of air. In future, it will know what to do.

Dolphins can swim at speeds of up to 40kph (25mph).

Fun and games

Dolphins are fast swimmers and amazing acrobats. Their speed helps them catch fish, but they also love to play and perform tricks. They can jump right out of the sea.

Spinner dolphins can jump up to 3m (10ft) out of the water, and spin around as many as seven times in the air.

These bottlenose dolphins are taking a look around. This is called spy hopping.

Using echoes

Dolphins find their way in the sea by making sounds which send back echoes. They can then tell what's around them by listening to the echoes. This is called sonar. Dolphins also use sonar to catch fish.

A dolphin makes a clicking sound which travels through the water.

When the sound hits some fish, it bounces back as an echo.

The dolphin can tell where the fish are by how long the echo takes.

27

Deep down

The deep sea is a very dark, cold place where some of the strangest creatures in the world live. There are no plants in the deep sea, so all the fish are predators.

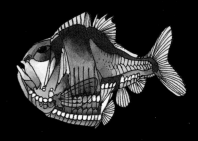

Hatchetfish have eyes on top of their heads so they can see fish which swim above them.

Internet link

At **www.usborne-quicklinks.com** you'll find a link to the **Seasky Web site**, where you can search the deep sea for monsters.

Gulper eels have enormous mouths. They can eat animals which are much larger than themselves.

Vampire squid

Vampire squid live as deep as 900m (3,000 feet). Their big eyes help them see in the murky depths.

Vampire squid have a clever way of escaping from predators. They can turn themselves inside out. The undersides of their tentacles are covered in sharp spikes, to stop other animals from eating them.

Vampire squid escape from predators by putting their tentacles over their heads.

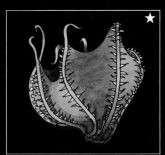

Their tentacles cover their bodies, making a spiky shield which protects them.

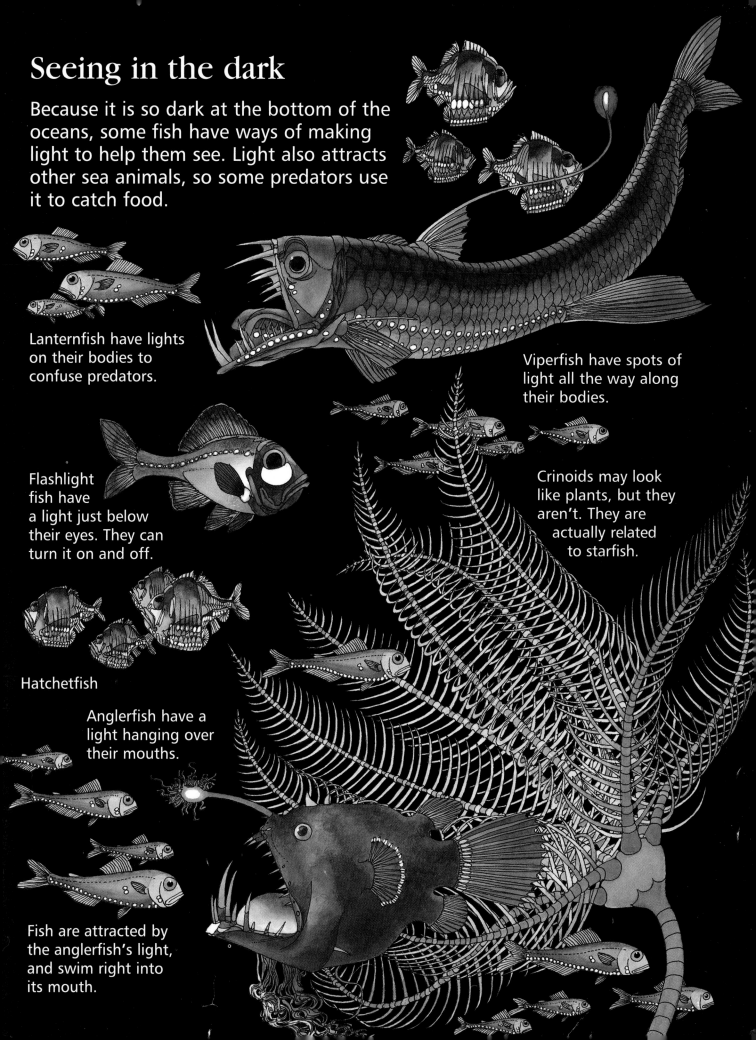

Seeing in the dark

Because it is so dark at the bottom of the oceans, some fish have ways of making light to help them see. Light also attracts other sea animals, so some predators use it to catch food.

Lanternfish have lights on their bodies to confuse predators.

Viperfish have spots of light all the way along their bodies.

Flashlight fish have a light just below their eyes. They can turn it on and off.

Crinoids may look like plants, but they aren't. They are actually related to starfish.

Hatchetfish

Anglerfish have a light hanging over their mouths.

Fish are attracted by the anglerfish's light, and swim right into its mouth.

On the move

Some sea animals have to make long journeys. They do this to find food, or to give birth. It is called migrating.

Wandering whales

Some whales migrate to the cold oceans in summer because the water there is full of krill, a kind of plankton which they can eat. In winter, they return to the warmer oceans to have their babies.

Humpback whales

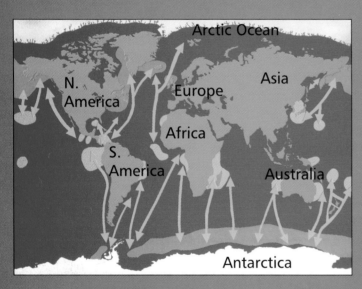

Humpback whales migrate. Some of them travel more that 16,000 km (10,000 miles) every year.

The arrows on this map show how far humpback whales travel each year.

Summer   Winter

Up and down

Some sea animals migrate every day. Copepods are a kind of plankton which stay in the deep sea during the day, but swim up to the surface at night to feed.

Copepods

This copepod is shown larger than it really is. Copepods are actually difficult to see, because they are so small.

Turtle travels

When she is ready to lay eggs, a female turtle goes back to the beach where she was born.

She makes a hole in the sand with her flippers. She lays her eggs in it and covers them with sand.

7 to 10 weeks later, baby turtles hatch from the eggs. They make their way down to the sea.

Years later, when they are fully-grown, the female turtles return to the same beach to lay their own eggs.

Eel adventures

Freshwater eels live in rivers until they are ready to lay eggs. Then they swim to the Sargasso Sea in the middle of the Atlantic Ocean to lay their eggs and die.

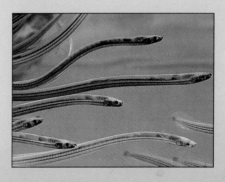

Baby eels, called elvers, swim back to the river that their parents came from. This can take as long as 3 years.

Internet link

At **www.usborne-quicklinks.com** you'll find a link to the **ABC Web site**, where you can learn all about turtles.

Salmon journeys

Salmon spend their lives in the ocean, but they always return to the part of the river where they were born to lay eggs.

Salmon have to swim up rivers and jump up waterfalls to get back to their birthplace.

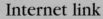

Cold oceans

The Arctic and Antarctic oceans are always cold. The surface of these oceans is frozen for most of the year, but the water under the ice is full of life.

Antarctic icefish have special liquid in their blood, to stop it from freezing.

Icy problem

Weddell seals hunt for food under the ice, but they have to come to the surface to breathe.

This weddell seal has made a breathing hole through the ice.

It scrapes at the ice with its sharp teeth, to keep the hole open.

Walruses

Walruses are mammals that live on land and in the sea. They have a layer of fatty blubber under their skins which keeps them warm.

These big teeth are called tusks.

Walruses feed in the water. They eat clams, which live on the seabed.

Penguins

Seven different kinds of penguins live in the Antarctic. Lots of birds could not live in such a cold and icy place, but penguins have found ways of surviving the freezing conditions.

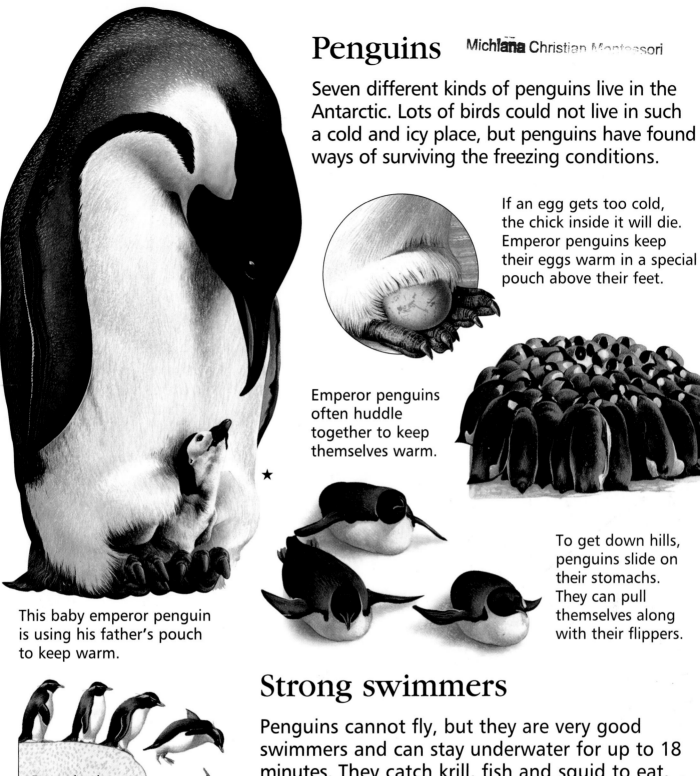

If an egg gets too cold, the chick inside it will die. Emperor penguins keep their eggs warm in a special pouch above their feet.

Emperor penguins often huddle together to keep themselves warm.

This baby emperor penguin is using his father's pouch to keep warm.

To get down hills, penguins slide on their stomachs. They can pull themselves along with their flippers.

Strong swimmers

Penguins cannot fly, but they are very good swimmers and can stay underwater for up to 18 minutes. They catch krill, fish and squid to eat.

Penguins jump, or dive into the sea from the ice.

Penguins use their webbed feet to swim fast underwater.

Penguins often jump out of the water to take a breath.

Sometimes they swim along the surface of the water, like ducks.

33

Waves

Waves are made far out at sea by the wind. They sometimes travel enormous distances across the oceans before finally crashing onto the seashore.

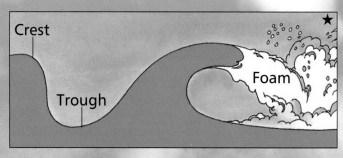

This picture shows what the different parts of a wave are called.

Making waves

Wind blowing across the sea makes ripples on the water. If the wind continues to blow, the ripples will get bigger and bigger, until they turn into waves.

When the wind blows across the top of waves it creates foam on them and makes them grow.

Breaking waves

The shape of a wave is affected by the depth of the sea. This makes waves change shape as they get closer to the coast.

Find out more

At **www.usborne-quicklinks.com** you'll find a link to the **Brainpop Web site**, where you can see a short movie about waves.

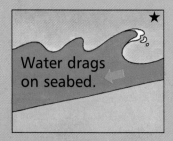

As a wave gets closer to land, the water gets shallower. The bottom part of the wave starts to drag on the seabed and slows down.

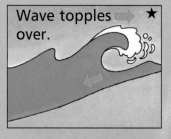

The top of the wave now moves faster than the bottom. This makes the top of the wave fall forward and topple over. This is called breaking.

Underwater energy

Waves are a kind of energy, moving through the water. Although the wave moves through the water, the water actually stays in the same place.

  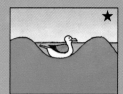

If you watch a wave, it looks as if the water moves along, but it doesn't.

When a wave passes under something such as a seagull, it just lifts it up.

When the wave has passed, the seagull is still in the same place as it was before.

Monster waves

The size of a wave depends on how strongly the wind is blowing and the distance it has covered. During storms at sea, strong winds create huge, powerful waves, which are big enough to sink a ship.

In some places, waves can be over 12m (40ft) high. That's higher than a two-floor house.

Currents

Currents are like big rivers which flow through the oceans. Different currents flow at different speeds. Some only move 10km (7 miles) a day. Others move up to 160km (100 miles) a day.

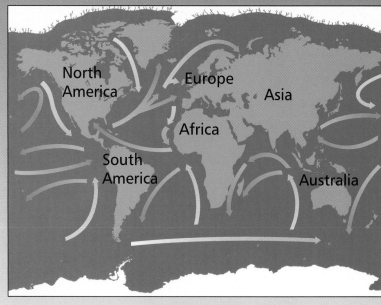

This map shows the world's main currents.

Warm current   Cold current

Carried by currents

Plant seeds are sometimes carried a very long way by a current. The new plant can grow a long distance away from its parent.

Internet link

At **www.usborne-quicklinks.com** you'll find a link to the **Ocean Currents Web site**, where you can find out the names of all the different currents.

Plant seeds, such as this coconut, fall in the sea. The current carries them away.

The seed sometimes travels for long distances before nearing land.

Waves carry the seed onto the shore. It may put down roots and grow.

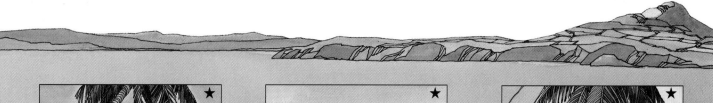
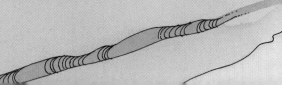

Tides

The height of the sea is called sea level. The sea level in most places is constantly changing through the day as the sea moves up and down the beach. This movement is called the tide.

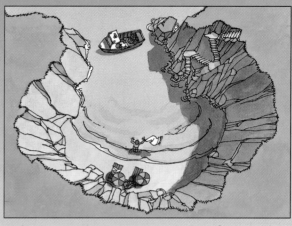

Tides sometimes come in very fast and trap people on beaches.

Tidelines

When the water reaches its highest point on a beach, it leaves a line of things from the sea behind. Then it starts to move back down the beach again. This line is called a tideline.

Seagulls look through tidelines, eating pieces of food they find.

There is often lots of seaweed left behind when the tide goes out.

The bones of cuttlefish, called cuttlebones, are often washed up on beaches by the tide.

This is a dogfish egg case. It is called a mermaid's purse.

Coasts

Coasts are the places where the land meets the sea. Coasts are always changing shape as waves and the wind wear them away.

Waves throw pebbles and rocks against the coast. Over time, this wears it away.

Bigger stones are at the back of the beach.

Small stones and sand are near the sea.

Making beaches

Beaches form on low, flat parts of the coast. Waves grind down big rocks and cliffs into smaller stones and pebbles, and finally into sand.

Sand is made up of billions of tiny stones, which have been worn down by waves.

Changing coasts

Some parts of a coast are made of harder rock than others. These parts are worn away more slowly by the sea, and form a headland.

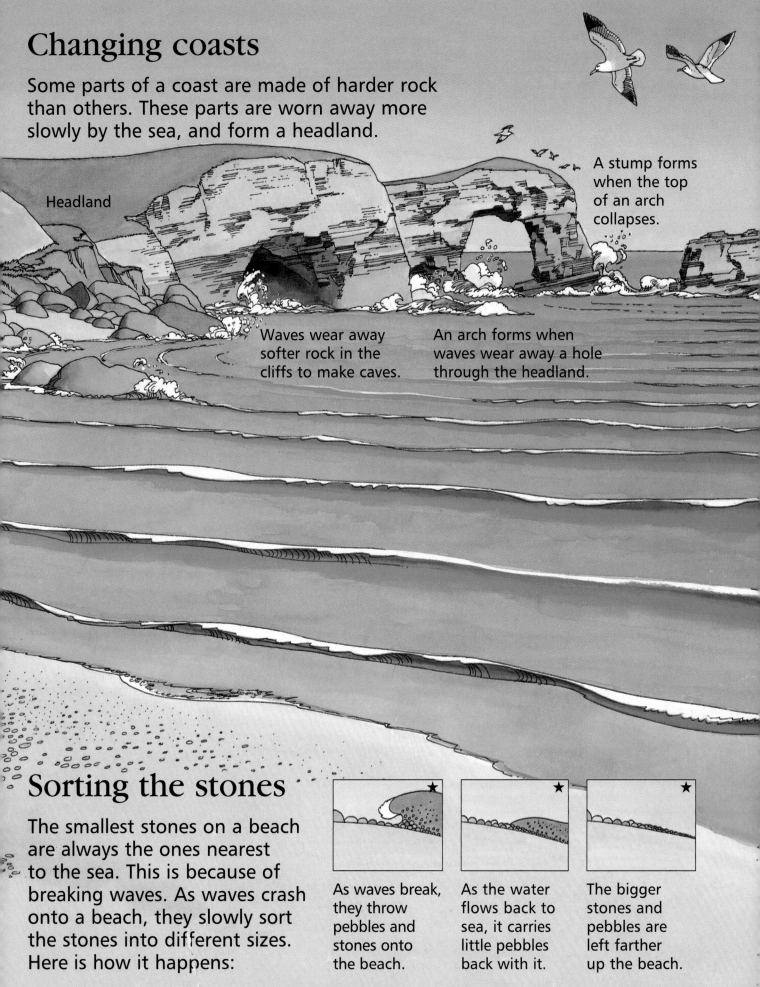

Headland

A stump forms when the top of an arch collapses.

Waves wear away softer rock in the cliffs to make caves.

An arch forms when waves wear away a hole through the headland.

Sorting the stones

The smallest stones on a beach are always the ones nearest to the sea. This is because of breaking waves. As waves crash onto a beach, they slowly sort the stones into different sizes. Here is how it happens:

As waves break, they throw pebbles and stones onto the beach.

As the water flows back to sea, it carries little pebbles back with it.

The bigger stones and pebbles are left farther up the beach.

Seashore life

There are lots of things to spot on the seashore. Every day when the tide goes out, it leaves pools of water trapped among the rocks. Plants and animals make their homes in these pools.

Five-bearded rocklings use feelers around their mouths to find their way.

Shrimp keep the water clean, eating anything they can find.

Butterfish have flat, slippery bodies. This helps them squeeze into gaps in the rocks, to hide from predators.

Blennies have large front fins which they use to change direction quickly in small pools.

Outside skeletons

A crab doesn't have a shell, but it has its skeleton on the outside. The skeleton is called a carapace. When the crab grows too big for its carapace, it wriggles out of it. Then its skin slowly hardens to make a new, bigger carapace.

Seaweed grows all along the seashore.

Crab

Mussels

Upside down

Barnacles cover the rocks along the seashore. They feed by sticking their legs out of the tops of their shells.

Tiny barnacles cling to the rocks in big groups. Their tough shells protect them from danger.

Barnacles open the tops of their shells to feed. Their legs stick out to pick up bits of food in the water.

Internet link

At **www.usborne-quicklinks.com** you'll find a link to the **Barnacles Web page**, where you can click on "How barnacles eat" to watch a short movie.

Special air bubbles keep this seaweed floating near the surface of the water, where it is light.

Sea scorpions are fierce predators. Their huge mouths can open wide enough to swallow large prey whole.

Starfish have five arms. If they lose an arm, another one grows in its place.

Hermit crab

Sea urchins have sharp spines on their shells to protect them.

Sea lemons scrape food off the rocks with their tongues.

Strawberry anemones

Limpets

Barnacles

Dog whelk

Dangerous seas

The weather at sea changes quickly. Violent storms and huge waves appear suddenly and can cause terrible damage.

Hurricanes

Hurricanes are violent storms which form over warm seas. Some hurricanes are so big they can be seen from space. Black clouds, heavy rain, huge waves and winds moving at speeds of up to 480kph (300mph) make hurricanes terrifying.

This is a picture of a hurricane taken from space. The spot in the middle, called the eye of the hurricane, is completely calm.

Waterspouts stretch from the sea all the way up to the clouds.

Waterspouts

Big storms sometimes pull water from the ocean up into a huge, spinning column called a waterspout. Waterspouts move across the ocean, sucking up anything in their path.

Sometimes waterspouts suck up fish and other sea animals. These drop back into the sea when the waterspout dies down.

Tsunami

Earthquakes make the ground move. When they happen under the sea they shake the seabed. This sometimes creates big, powerful waves. These waves are called tsunami (say soonarmee).

When an earthquake happens under the sea, part of the seabed rises or falls.

The movement of the seabed moves the sea above, making long, low tsunami waves.

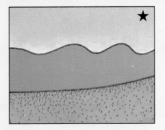

The waves move out fast in all directions from the place where they were made.

If tsunami reach the coast, they are squeezed up into huge, tall waves.

Wave of destruction

In the deep ocean, tsunami are not dangerous. They are low waves which may pass under ships without anybody noticing. Tsunami only become enormous when they reach shallow water. Then they break and crash down onto the land, destroying everything in their way.

★ The biggest tsunami ever recorded was 34m (112ft) high. That's bigger than a ten-floor building.

Internet link

At **www.usborne-quicklinks.com** you'll find a link to **Hurricane Harry's Web site**, where you can find out more about hurricanes.

Boats and ships

Boats were invented thousands of years ago. They help people move things from one place to another, and to explore the world around them.

Funnel

Cruise ships are like floating hotels. They sometimes have swimming pools and tennis courts on them. ★

Lifeboats like this can be used in emergencies.

A ship's back is called its stern.

4 propellers push the ship forward.

4 engines power the propellers.

Internet link

At **www.usborne-quicklinks.com** you'll find a link to the **Thinkquest Adventures at Sea Web site**, where you can go to a sailor school.

First boats

The first boats were small. They were made by hollowing out logs. Later, people built bigger boats and ships.

★
The first boats were hollowed out logs. They were heavy, and hard to use.

★

Later, people made lighter boats by stretching animal skins around sticks.

★
The first big boats were rowing boats, called galleys. This is a Greek galley.

Wind power

Sailing ships had lots of huge sails instead of oars. The sails filled up with wind which pushed the ships along. When there was no wind, the ships could not go anywhere.

This kind of sailing ship is called a galleon. Galleons were used about 400 years ago.

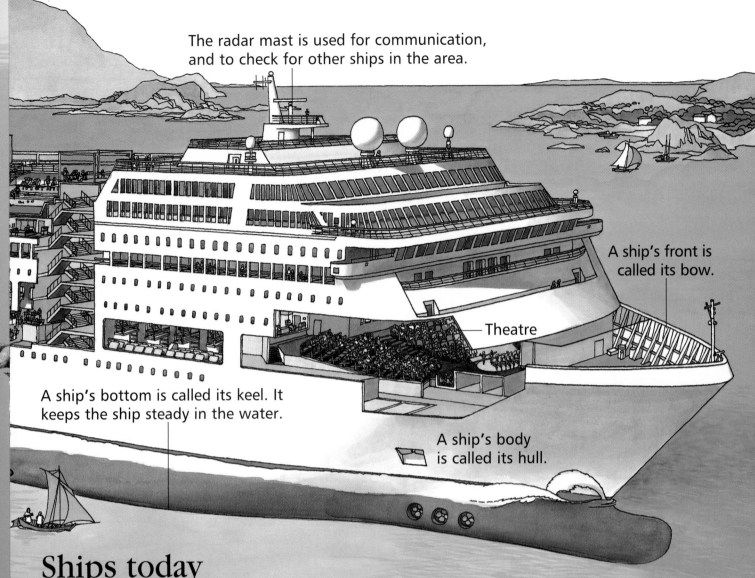

The radar mast is used for communication, and to check for other ships in the area.

A ship's front is called its bow.

Theatre

A ship's bottom is called its keel. It keeps the ship steady in the water.

A ship's body is called its hull.

Ships today

Ships today can be much bigger than the ships of the past. They are used to move things, such as fuel and food, from one place to another all over the world. People also relax on huge cruise ships, such as the one shown above. Small fast boats are sometimes used for travel.

Oil tankers are ships for carrying oil. They can be over 1km (½ mile) long. Some are so big, people on them use bicycles to get around.

A hovercraft can move very quickly. A big cushion of air underneath it makes it fly just above the surface of the sea.

Shipwrecks

Ships which have sunk are called shipwrecks. Some shipwrecks are hundreds of years old. This is a Spanish galleon, which sank more than 400 years ago.

Divers exploring shipwreck

Breathing tank

Mask for seeing underwater

Flippers help the diver swim faster.

This diver is drawing the wreck using waterproof paper, and a pen which works underwater.

Exploring shipwrecks

Divers often explore shipwrecks. They wear tanks on their backs, filled with air. They breathe the air through a tube. This means they can stay underwater for a long time.

Sea animals, such as this moray eel, make their homes in nooks and crannies in the wreck.

Divers use special balloons filled with air to take things from the wreck up to the surface.

These divers have found a cannon on the galleon. They are taking it up to the surface.

Over time, coral and plants grow on shipwrecks. This makes them difficult to find.

Some ships carrying treasure have been wrecked. Lots of the treasure has never been found.

Artifacts

Man-made things found in shipwrecks are called artifacts. Artifacts often help us learn about how people lived in the past.

These urns come from a wreck in Turkey. The wreck is more than 1,000 years old.

These gold bars were found on a sunken galleon called the *Santa Margerita*.

This is a plate from the *Titanic*, which sank in 1912 when it hit an iceberg.

49

Using the oceans

The oceans are very important to us in many ways. We need them to help us survive. We get food and energy from them. They also give us minerals and medicines.

These fishermen in India are throwing out their nets. They hope to catch some fish in them.

Big nets

Fishermen use nets of various sizes to catch fish. Some, like the one above, can only catch a few fish at a time. The huge nets pulled by ships can catch thousands at once. These nets are up to 2km (a mile) long.

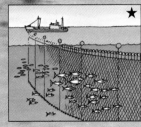

Drift nets hang from the surface. They trap fish that try to swim through them.

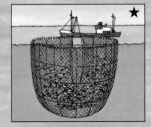

Purse seine nets are like big bags. They catch herring and other fish near the surface.

Trawl nets drag along the sea bed. They catch fish such as plaice that live on the bottom.

Drilling for oil

In some of the rocks under the seabed, there is lots of oil. Big companies use oil rigs to drill holes into the seabed and get it out. It is used as fuel for things such as cars, factories and power stations.

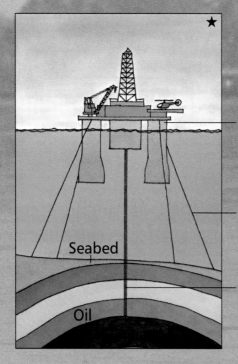

★ Floating oil rig

These floats stop the rig from sinking.

Cables with anchors on them stop the rig from moving.

Seabed

Oil

This pipe goes into the seabed as far as the oil. The oil is then pumped up.

Food, jewels and medicines

We get a lot more than just food and energy from the oceans. Here are some of the other things that come from the sea.

Mother-of-pearl covers the inside of abalone shells. It is used to decorate things.

★

Pearls are found inside animals called oysters. They are used to make necklaces and earrings.

★

★ Some kinds of seaweed are good to eat. Seaweed is also used to make shampoo and ice cream.

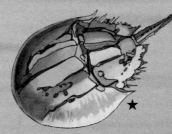

★ Some medicines come from the sea. Horseshoe crabs' blood is used to test for diseases.

51

Dirty oceans

The oceans are getting dirtier and dirtier because of things people dump in them. Our waste kills sea plants and animals. Here are some of the different ways people harm the oceans.

In some places, sewage pipes take waste from bathrooms and toilets and dump it into the sea.

Many farmers use chemicals to help their crops grow. When it rains, some of the chemicals are washed into rivers, and then into the sea.

Plastic dumped in the sea can take longer than 80 years to rot away.

Some ships dump their litter into the sea.

Some people leave litter behind on beaches. When the tide comes in, it is washed out to sea.

Oil spills

Huge oil tankers sometimes hit rocks or crash into other ships and oil leaks out into the sea. This can harm the sea and the animals that live in it.

Internet link

At **www.usborne-quicklinks.com** you'll find a link to the **Secrets at Sea Web site**, where you can become a detective and solve an environmental mystery.

Seabirds get oil stuck in their feathers. When they try to clean it off with their beaks, it poisons them.

Some spilled oil floats on top of the water.

Oil tankers carry enormous amounts of oil. A big oil spill can cover a huge area.

When oil washes up on beaches, it sticks to the sand and pebbles and kills the plants and animals along the seashore.

Cleaning up

Cleaning up after an oil spill is a difficult job. People have to catch and clean the oily animals. Then they release them away from the oil.

This oil-covered seal is being cleaned with dishwashing liquid.

Emptying the oceans

As well as making the oceans dirty, we damage them in other ways. When we take too much from the oceans, it puts the animals and plants that live in them in danger.

Overfishing

When fishermen catch too many of the same kind of fish, the number in the sea starts to go down. This is called overfishing.

Modern fishing boats make catching fish much easier than it used to be.

Fishermen use helicopters to look for schools of fish.

Fishing controls

Some countries try to control the problem of overfishing. They make fishermen use special nets which only catch the larger fish.

The big holes in this fishing net allow small fish to escape.

Fish in danger

These fish are all in danger from overfishing. If fishermen don't stop catching them soon, they will die out completely.

More than 100 million sharks are caught each year. Their fins are used to make soup. The rest is thrown away.

Small fish, such as haddock, are overfished.

Cod can grow up to 1.5m (5ft) long, but there are almost no big cod left, because of overfishing.

Pacific salmon have been overfished.

Millions of bigeye tuna are caught each year to make a Japanese food called sushi.

Coral in danger

Coral reefs are being damaged all over the world. Reefs grow slowly. Every reef that people damage will take hundreds of years to grow again.

★ Fishermen use poison to catch tropical fish from reefs. They sell them to pet shops.

People take coral to make things such as necklaces.

Coral is often damaged by careless divers.

Getting warmer

The temperature of the Earth is changing. When fuels such as coal and oil are burned to make energy, they warm the air around them. As it gets warmer, the sea level rises.

Heated atmosphere

The Earth is surrounded by a blanket of gases called the atmosphere. This traps heat and air around the Earth making it possible for life to exist. The atmosphere also stops the extra heat we make from escaping into space. As the atmosphere gets warmer, it heats up the land and the seas. ★

The Sun's rays warm the Earth.

The atmosphere stops some of the heat from escaping.

Sun's heat

Power stations burn coal to make electricity.

Piles of waste give off gases which warm the atmosphere.

Forests are burned. The land is turned into fields.

Some of the heat we make escapes back into space but some gets trapped in the atmosphere. This warms the planet.

Cars burn fuel, and produce exhaust, which warms the air.

The problem of the Earth heating up is called global warming.

Melting ice

As the atmosphere warms up, the ice in the Arctic and Antarctic starts to melt. The water goes back into the oceans, making the sea level rise.

The air gets warmer. Ice melts into the sea. The sea level rises.

Rising seas

If all the ice in the world melted, it would cause a worldwide disaster. The sea level everywhere would rise by more than 60m (200ft). To stop this from happening, we need to find ways of making energy without burning fuels such as oil and coal. Find out more on the next page.

This picture shows what would happen to a town by the sea if the sea level rose by 60m (200ft).

Some islands in the sea would be flooded if all the ice melted.

Internet link

At **www.usborne-quicklinks.com** you'll find a link to the **Global Warming Web site**, where you can play games and learn about global warming.

As ice melts at the poles, huge chunks of it fall into the sea.

The future of the oceans

Fuels, such as oil, may one day run out, and anyway, using them harms the Earth. But there are ways of getting energy from the sea itself. In the future, we could get most of our energy from the sea, and even live in it.

Wind power

The surface of the sea is often windy. Big windmills, called wind turbines, could be attached to the seabed and used to make electricity from the wind.

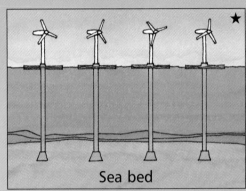

Sea bed

Wind blowing across the sea turns the windmill blades.

The spinning blades power a machine called a turbine inside the windmill, which makes electricity.

Water power

This bridge in France is also a power station. It is built across an estuary (a place where a river meets the sea). As the tide comes in and out it turns wheels under the water, which make electricity.

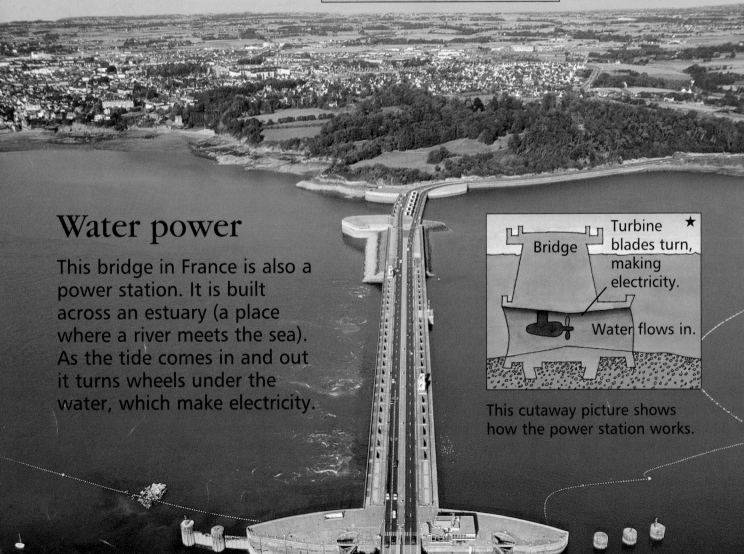

Bridge

Turbine blades turn, making electricity.

Water flows in.

This cutaway picture shows how the power station works.

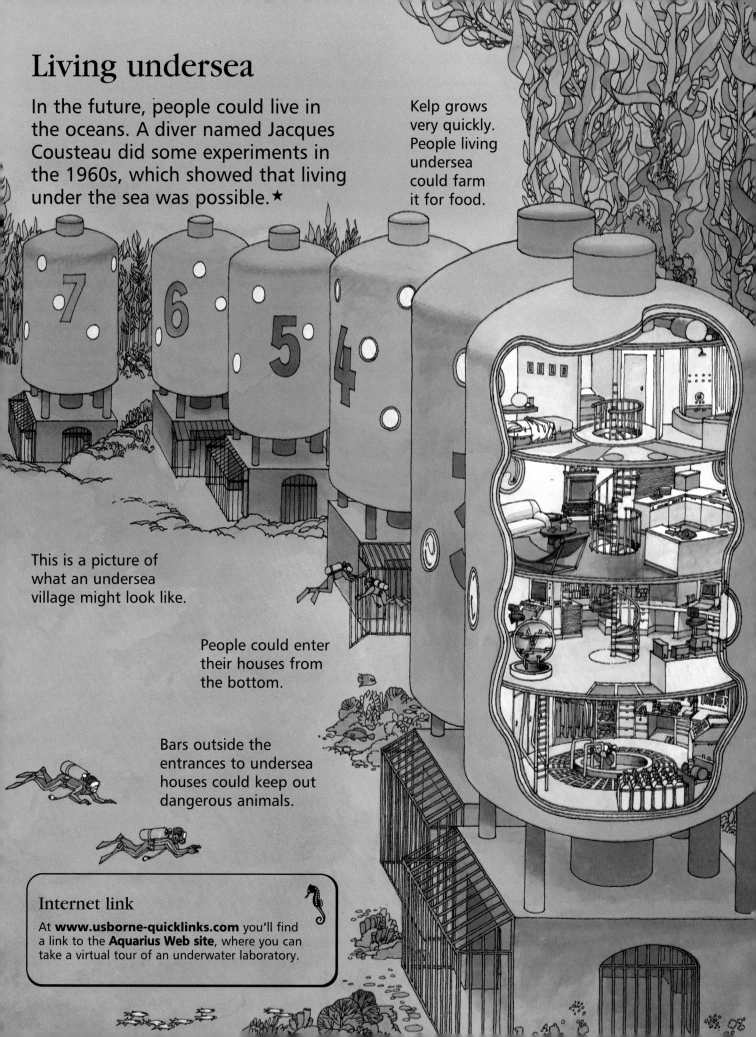

Living undersea

In the future, people could live in the oceans. A diver named Jacques Cousteau did some experiments in the 1960s, which showed that living under the sea was possible. ★

Kelp grows very quickly. People living undersea could farm it for food.

This is a picture of what an undersea village might look like.

People could enter their houses from the bottom.

Bars outside the entrances to undersea houses could keep out dangerous animals.

Internet link

At **www.usborne-quicklinks.com** you'll find a link to the **Aquarius Web site**, where you can take a virtual tour of an underwater laboratory.

Undersea facts and records

The sea animals with the biggest eyes are giant squid. Their eyes are the size ★ of basketballs.

The biggest coral reef in the world is the Great Barrier Reef off the east coast of Australia. It is so big, that it can be seen from space.

Giant kelp are the fastest growing plants in the world. They grow up to 60cm (24in) each day.

The slowest swimming sea creature is the dwarf seahorse. It would take one 2 days to swim 1km (½mile).

The fastest fish in the sea is the sailfish. It can swim at incredible speeds of up to 110kph (70mph).

The smallest fish in the sea is the dwarf goby. A fully-grown dwarf goby is less than 1cm (½in) long.

Pacific giant octopuses can grow to enormous sizes. The tentacles of a fully-grown giant octopus can measure over 2m (7ft) long.

★ Blue whales are the biggest animals that have ever lived. They grow up to 33m (110ft) long. That's longer than a tennis court.

Dolphins have amazing hearing. They hear sounds through a special bone in their lower jaw.

Box jellyfish have deadly poisonous tentacles. Their poison could kill a person in under 4 minutes.

★ Emperor penguins are excellent swimmers and can stay underwater for up to 18 minutes.

Diatoms are a kind of plankton. Their shells are used to make dynamite.

Killer whales are black on top so that prey swimming above them can't see them against the dark depths.

★ Flying fish escape from predators by jumping out of the sea. They can glide for over 1km (½ mile).

Pufferfish contain a deadly poison called tetradetoxin. One drop of tetradetoxin could kill a person.

Average sizes

★
Giant octopus 2m (7ft) long

★
Dolphin 2.5m (8ft) long

★
Killer whale 7m (23ft) long

★
Giant squid 18m (60ft) long

★
Blue whale 30m (99ft) long

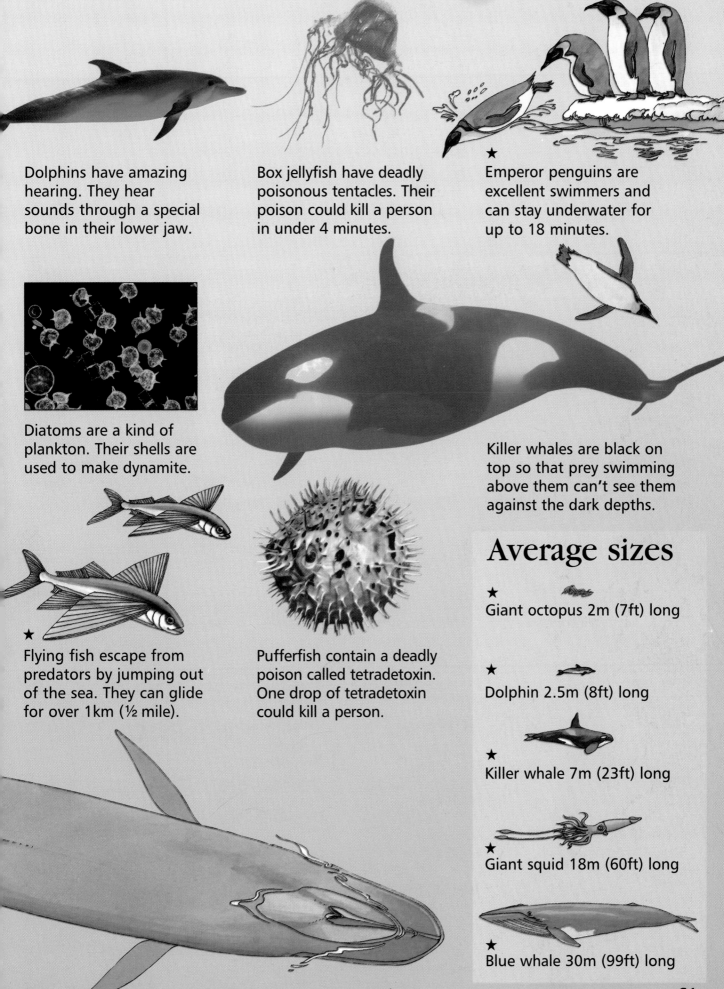

Index

abalone shells, 51
anemones, 13, 16
      strawberry, 41
Antarctic Ocean, 5, 32, 33, 57
arches, 39
Arctic Ocean, 5, 32, 57
artifacts, 49
Atlantic Ocean, 5

bacteria, 9
barnacles, 25, 41
beaches, 38
boats 44, 45
brittle stars, 12

camouflage, 10
caves, 39
clams, giant, 13
cliffs, 39
coal, 56, 57
coasts, 4, 38, 39
coelacanths, 47
cone shells, 18
continental shelf, 4
corals, 12, 13
      brain, 12
coral animals, 12, 13, 14, 15
coral reefs, 6, 12, 13, 14, 15, 17, 55, 60
crabs, 40
      hermit, 41
      horseshoe, 51
crinoids, 29
crittercams, 46
cruise ships 44, 45
currents, 36
cuttlebones, 37
cuttlefish, 11, 37

Deep Flight submersible, 46
divers, 4, 20, 23, 48, 55
dog whelks, 41
dolphins, 6, 26, 27, 61
      bottlenose, 27
      spinner, 27

earthquakes, 43

eels, 12
      elvers, 31
      freshwater, 31
      gulper, 28
      moray, 17, 48
estuaries, 58

feather stars, 13
fish, 7
      angelfish, 12, 14
      anglerfish, 29
      bigeye tuna, 55
      blennies, 40
      boxfish, 15
      butterfish, 40
      butterfly fish, 15
      cleanerfish, 17
      clownfish, 16
      clown triggerfish, 14
      cod, 55
      coelacanths, 47
      crescent-tailed bigeye fish, 15
      dwarf gobies, 60
      five-bearded rocklings, 40
      flashlight fish, 29
      flying fish, 61
      gobies, 17
      groupers, 17
         giant, 14
      haddock, 55
      hatchetfish, 28
      herring, 9
      icefish, Antarctic, 32
      lanternfish, 29
      lionfish, 18
      mackerel, 8, 9
      oarfish, 47
      parrotfish, 13
      pearlfish, 16
      pufferfish, 15, 61
      rabbitfish, 18
      remoras, 16
      sailfish, 60
      salmon, 31
         Pacific, 55
      sargassum frogfish, 11

sea scorpions, 41
shrimpfish, 11
stonefish, 18
tuna, 9
viperfish, 29
fishermen, 50, 55
fishing nets, 50

galleons, 44
galleys, 44
giant clams, 13
giant kelp, 60
giant squid, 47, 60, 61
Great Barrier Reef, 60

headlands, 39
helicopters, 54
hovercraft, 45
hurricanes, 42, 43

Indian Ocean, 5
islands, 5

jellyfish,
	box, 18, 61
	porpita, 19

kelp, 59, 60

limpets, 41
living undersea, 59

Mariana Trench, 5
mermaid's purse, 37
migration, 30
mother-of-pearl, 51
mussels, 40

nutrients, 9

octopuses, 14
	blue-ringed, 18
	Pacific giant, 60, 61
oil, 4, 51, 53, 56, 57, 58
oil rigs, 4, 51
oil tankers, 45, 53
overfishing, 54, 55

Pacific Ocean, 5
pearls, 51

penguins, 33
	emperor, 33, 61
Petronas Towers, 5
plankton, 8, 23, 30
	copepods, 30
	diatoms, 8, 61
	phytoplankton, 8, 9
	zooplankton, 8, 9
poison, 6, 18, 19, 55
Portuguese man-of-war, 18
power stations, 56, 58

rays, 22, 23
	electric, 22
	manta, 22, 23
	stingrays, 22

sailing ships, 44
salmon, 31
	Pacific, 55
Santa Margerita, 49
Sargasso Sea, 31
schools, 15
seabed, 4
seabirds, 53
	seagulls, 37
seahorses, 14
	dwarf, 60
seals, 32, 53
sea dragons, 10
sea fans, 12
sea lemons, 41
sea level, 37, 56, 57
sea slugs, 6, 19
sea snakes, 19
sea urchins, 11, 12, 41
seaweed, 11, 37, 40, 41, 51, 59
	sargassum, 11
sewage, 52
sharks, 6, 19, 20, 55
	great white, 20
	hammerhead, 21
	megamouth, 47
	sand tiger, 21
	whale, 21
	wobbegong, 10
shipwrecks, 48
shrimps, 17, 40
	banded coral, 17
sponges, 12

squid
  giant, 47, 60, 61
  vampire, 28
starfish, 41
storms, 42
submersibles, 46
symbiosis, 16

tideline, 37
tides, 37, 58
Titanic, 49
treasure, 49
tsunami, 43
turtles, 31
  green, 16

volcanoes, 5

walruses, 32
waterspouts, 42
waves, 34
whales, 24, 25, 30
  blue, 24, 60, 61
  humpback, 9, 24, 25, 30
  killer, 8, 9, 61
  minke, 24
  right, 24
  sperm, 24, 25, 46
wind turbines, 58

Acknowledgements

The publishers are grateful to the following for permission to reproduce material.

Key

t = top, m=middle, b= bottom, l = left, r = right

Ardea London: 6ml (Francis Gohier), 10b (Kevin Deacon), 24-25t (Francois Gohier), 4mr (Peter Green), 61tm (Ron and Valerie Taylor). **Agents Frances Press:** 42bl. **BBC Natural History Unit Picture Library:** 30b (Sinclair Stammers), 60m (Avi Klapfer/Jeffrey L. Rotman), 60mr (David Hall), 60bl (Jeffrey L. Rotman), 61m (Hans Christoph Kappel). **Bruce Coleman Collection:** 1b (Richard Herman/Innerspace Visions), 6t, 15tl, 23, 25bl (Johnny Johnson), 23m, 32b (Hans Reinhard). **Corbis:** 5b (Steve Raymer), 8tl (Amos Nachoum), 8bl (Douglas P. Wilson/Frank Lane Picture Agency), 8br (Douglas P. Wilson/Frank Lane Picture Agency), 14tl (Tom Brakefield), 14ml (Robert Yin), 16t (Lawson Wood), 19b (Brandon D. Cole), 20-21 (Jeffrey L. Rotman), 20bl (Stuart Westmorland), 21br (Brandon D. Cole), 34ml (Gary Braasch), 42 (Bettmann), 45bl (Craig Aurness), 45br (Dean Conger), 49tr (Jonathan Blair), 49mr (Jonathan Blair), 49br (Ralph White), 52tr (Ian Harwood/Ecoscene), 53bl (George Lepp), 55tl (Amos Nachoum), 58b (Yann Arthur Betrand), 61ml (Douglas P. Wilson, Frank Lane Picture Agency), 61m (Stephen Frink). **Digital Vision:** 3br, 5b, 26tl, 30m, 35b, 36tr, 38bl, 61t. **Imagequest 3-D:** 19m (Peter Parks). **Innerspace Visions:** 47ml (Bruce Rasner). **Natural History Photographic Agency:** 14ml (Yves Lanceau), 46tr (Norbert Wu), 55tc (Kevin Schafer), 55l (Jeff Goodman), 60cl (B. Jones and M. Shimlock). **Oxford Scientific Films:** 31cl (Roger Jackman). **Phillip Colla:** 21tr (Philip Colla). **Popperfoto:** 53b (Daniel Joubert/Reuters). **Powerstock Zefa Ltd:** Cover, 31b. **Rudolf Svensen:** 55tc (Rudolf Svensen). **Still Pictures:** 6bl (Sergio Hanquet), 6br (Secret Sea Visions), 12tr (Alain Compost), 15b (Fred Bavenden), 16bl (Fred Bavenden), 21-22 (Norbert Wu), 27ml (Horst Schafer), 30tl (Yves Lefevre), 50-51 (Mike Schroder).

Additional llustrators:

Ian Jackson, John Woodcock, Chris Shields.